T0208219

The Helper

Monica Mangidza

WestBow
PRESS®
A DIVISION OF THOMAS NELSON
& ZONDERVAN

Scripture taken from the King James Version of the Bible

WestBow Press books may be ordered through booksellers or by contacting:

WestBow Press
A Division of Thomas Nelson & Zondervan
1663 Liberty Drive
Bloomington, IN 47403
www.westbowpress.com
1 (866) 928-1240

ISBN: 978-1-9736-5875-7 (sc)
ISBN: 978-1-9736-5876-4 (hc)
ISBN: 978-1-9736-5874-0 (e)

Library of Congress Control Number: 2019904048

Print information available on the last page.

WestBow Press rev. date: 04/29/2019

Have you ever wondered what exactly you are meant to do as a wife? Or maybe you knew it but your marriage isn't quite that picture-perfect story? In this booklet, Monica pours out her heart and shares some powerful insights on what it is to be a helper. I hope you are encouraged, excited, motivated, and empowered to be that helper God created you to be.

Monica Mangidza
A woman with a desire to teach and empower women of all ages and nations

Dedication

I dedicate this booklet to all women, especially girls. I specifically dedicate this to my only daughter, Nyengeterai, because she is a woman.

I also dedicate this booklet to my niece, Grace, for her unwavering support in the writing and production of this piece.

Acknowledgments

Though I, Monica Mangidza, wrote this booklet, I acknowledge that I received all this revelation from my pastors and teachers and their inspired words. I have learned at their feet and was drawn to become what I am from the day I was born again on December 24, 1980, in the Family of God church. I am sincerely grateful for their guidance.

I also thank all friends and family who helped and encouraged me. I appreciate their invaluable support.

Contents

Introduction

It is my sincere wish that as you read this, you will begin to want to know more about yourself and will realize the potential God has bestowed on you. You will not just accept what the world thinks a woman is; you will be more critical of issues pertaining to you as a woman because you know yourself best and you follow the principles God laid down for a helper.

Here is a simple example to illustrate the passiveness we women can be subject to. Is the underwear we wear daily the right cut for us? Is the gusset squarely where we want it to be? Is it as big and wide as is convenient for us?

The underwear we use today was probably designed by a man who by virtue of his sex can never personally appreciate a woman's structure and needs. Believe you me, gussets could be longer and bigger and hence more effective for us women. Why do we put on just what is available on the market? Is it really our nature as women to just accept what we are presented with without questioning?

In the following chapters, I will look at what the Bible says about wives in everyday life because it is not just a matter of being housewives; there is more to it than simply that.

Chapter 1

What Is a Helper?

Coming together is a beginning.
Keeping together is progress.
Working together is success.

This popular quote by Henry Ford is displayed in many homes and offices. I have added a few words to this famous quote to make it more relevant to marriage.

Coming together is a beginning.
Keeping together is progress.
Working together is success.
And dying together is victory.

Genesis 2:18 says, "And the Lord God said, It is not good that the man should be alone, I will make an help meet for him.[1]"

It was God's idea and initiative to create woman. He started marriage because he saw that it was not good for man to be alone. God made a helpmeet for man. He did not make a lesser human being, nor did he make a more superior being. He simply made man a helpmeet.

---

[1] All scriptural passages come from the King James Version of the Bible.

Who does not need help? We all at one point or another need helpers with chores at home, carrying heavy objects, and accomplishing many other tasks. When we are happy and excited, we need someone to share our happiness with. When we are low and sad, we again need helpers. Things like learning to ride a bicycle require physical helpers as do climbing mountains, replacing lightbulbs, threading needles, solving crossword puzzles, and even scratching our backs. We need helpers!

Ecclesiastes 4:9 says two are better than one. God had foreseen all this when he decided to make a helpmeet for man, and it was woman he made. In Genesis 2:21–23, we learn that God made a woman from Adam's rib. In verse 23, when Adam saw the woman, he declared, "This is now bone of my bones, and flesh of my flesh, she shall be called woman because she was taken out of man."

I am positive Adam also saw that it was good to have Eve around. He had someone who could scratch his back and was superior to the beasts of the field and the fowls of the air. He had someone he could relate to, who could understand him, and who was a part of him.

Let us again look at a helper. Anybody can help. A German shepherd can help farmers by looking after sheep. Dogs can help the blind walk safely. A young child can help an adult. An uneducated person can help a professor, and employees can help their employers. A helper can be anybody; lesser people can be effective helpers of greater people, and we all need help at one point or another.

Equally so in this instance, a man needed a helper who was designed to be a woman. Have you ever thought that a helper could be more intelligent than the person being helped? As a young student, when I needed help in mathematics, I would turn to those more gifted than I was. In some instances, we have to seek help from specialists because the problems we face can be beyond our abilities to solve.

When God made woman, he was glad because man was no longer alone. He had made man a special helper who was more like a soulmate. In Genesis 2:18, man had a partner. God's idea for man and woman was that they would help each other enjoy the earth. They would work together in the Garden of Eden. They would play together as did Isaac, who sported with his wife, Rebekah.

Every woman should step ahead with confidence and help the man in her life as was God's intention. God designed every woman with that purpose in mind.

As mentioned in Genesis 26:8, Isaac was playful with Rebekah, and that is what it should be like between husband and wife; they should be playful, happy, and affectionate with each other. Man and woman cannot sport with each other when they are not on speaking terms or are angry with each other.

Adam and Eve were happy together in the garden; they did not have any worries, and all was going well. God's initial plan and desire was for couples to share quality time and quality lives together.

Chapter 2

Helping Each Other Serve God

A woman should help a man serve God. In Luke 2:4–5, Caesar Augustus decreed that all people should be taxed. Joseph went up with his wife, Mary, though she was great with child. Glory! A helper does not stop the man of God from doing his duties; she encourages him all the way. It would have been easy for Mary to plead with Joseph for her not to go because she was heavy with child, but she did not. She was not a hindrance; that is one of the characteristics of a good helper. She went with him though that was inconvenient and uncomfortable.

In 1 Samuel 1:7, 10, Elkanah went to worship God year after year. Hannah went with him, and she prayed to the Lord as well. After many years of doing this, Hannah was blessed by giving birth to Samuel. She did not stop or give up before she got him. Helpers stand firm on promises and do things to make their companions comfortable in the house of God. A profitable helper does not do things only because all is well.

Elkanah had married a second wife, Peninnah, who had children, and Hannah did not have any. In 1 Samuel 1:6, we read, "And her adversary also provoked her sore for to make her fret because the Lord had shut her womb." That did not hinder Hannah from serving God. Instead, it encouraged her to dwell in the temple and talk to God. As it turned out, testing time was promotion time. God heard her and blessed her with Samuel.

Hannah, Sarah, and many others were dedicated helpers. Even after Elkanah had married another wife, Hanna dwelt there. I believe deep down in their hearts that as helpers, they prayed for the will of God to come into their lives. For sure, the Lord blessed Hannah and Sarah with sons. That, however, didn't come automatically.

I am positive God was moved by their faith and dedication to their husbands.

Delilah was one helper who was not flowing together with the man she should have been helping. She was on her own mission, which was contrary to what the man thought (Judges 16, 17, 19). Delilah pressed Samson with her words daily and vexed his soul until he let the cat out of the bag. Delilah shaved Samson's hair. That led to the Philistines capturing him, and that led to his death.

Job had been inflicted with sores by Satan from the soles of his feet to the crown of his head. In Job 2:9, we hear the wife saying, "Dost thou still retain thine integrity? Curse God and die." These words came to a man who was in intense pain. It would have been easy to curse God, but Job was perfect and upright, and he eschewed evil. Consequently, he did not curse his God. The helpers in these instances were not good helpers. Helpers seek to do their husbands good all the days of their lives (Proverbs 31:1–2).

It is also vital to note that Job's wife had to nurse him throughout his sickness. A helper has to be practical and make do with what is available. All ended well for this family. They were later blessed by the Lord, and they had ten more children. Their daughters turned out to be the fairest in the land.

Proverbs 21:9 says, "It is better to dwell in a corner of the house top than with a brawling woman in a wide house." We see that it was not only Samson who could not handle a woman of many words; not all men can. So a helper should be full of wisdom. She should use words with expertise and wisdom.

A God-fearing helper should always seek to do God's will and therefore should know what the Word of God says for each time and situation she is in, which vary. A good helper should be able to say as the psalmist in Psalm 51:10 did, "Create in me a clean heart oh God and renew a right spirit within me." This is especially vital when confronted with difficult and unpleasant situations.

A helper should stay focused and never lose sight of what her God-ordained duties are: to do the man good all the days of her life (Proverbs

31:12)! There is always a success story when a woman takes her role and stands with her husband as an honest helper.

In the book of Ruth, Naomi was married to Elimelech, who died and left her and their two grown-up sons. Even after Elimelech's death, Naomi continued as a helper. Naomi was concerned about the welfare of her daughters-in-law such that in Ruth 1:12–13, she told Ruth and Orpah that she could not keep them as daughters-in-law as she was aged and unable to bear other sons to marry them. The family did not disintegrate because Elimelech had died. The helper, Naomi, was there.

Naomi was a committed helper. She felt she owed it to her daughters-in-law. She wanted them to remarry and start their lives over again, but Ruth refused to go. Of the two daughters-in-law, Ruth was more committed to Naomi than was Orpah. The fruits of commitment were witnessed shortly after Ruth got married to Boaz, who was a mighty man of wealth (Ruth 2:1).

The helper honors her vows. Hannah vowed to God in 1 Samuel 1:11 that if God looked on her affliction, remembered her, and gave her a son, she would give him to the Lord. The Lord remembered her, and in turn, she kept her vow and gave Samuel back to the Lord.

When you get married, you make personal and legal vows in front of God and all people who gather to be witnesses. God expects us to fulfill our vows. Are these words familiar?

I invite all of you present to witness that I _____ take you _____ to be my lawfully wedded husband, to be with me, to live with me from this day onward, through good times and bad times, through richness, through poverty, in sickness and in health, to love you only, till death do us part according to the holy statutes of God. Therefore, I give you this ring as my promise.

Do we as helpers still adhere to what we promised we would do when we married? It is a sin to break vows. Naomi strived to keep her family intact, and so must we as helpers. We are not to be agents of the devil whom he uses to break families apart.

A helper should be a person of integrity. She should be a trustworthy person, a firm and honest woman, because she is like a person steering a boat. She will have to make judgments and decisions promptly, and any miscalculation could be fatal. This is evident in Acts 5, the story about Ananias and Sapphira, who connived to lie. They did not remember they were lying to God, who sees and knows everything even if it is done secretly. The result was that husband and wife died. Sapphira, the helper, had failed her duties; she did not lift up her husband.

Sarah was Abraham's helper. In Genesis 18:7, Abraham went into the tent to Sarah and asked her to prepare quickly three measures of fine meal, knead it, and make cakes on the hearth, which Sarah did. I presume Abraham knew that Sarah was very good at that. A helper's strengths should be well known. Sarah was a keeper of the home; she made Abraham comfortable. A helper should run the affairs of the home extremely well for the well-being of the whole family.

In Genesis 29:9, Rachel came to the well to water the sheep. She helped in that regard; from time immemorial, men and women have helped each other with chores. In this instance, a woman was helping a man by looking after the livestock. In this case, Rachael was looking after her father's sheep.

Chapter 3

A Practical Woman

𝒫roverbs 31 outlines some of the tasks a helper should perform; unfortunately, the devil through culture has shrouded the duties of a woman as she helps a man. A woman can produce things of substance as evidenced by the following.

In Proverbs 31:13, a woman is in the manufacturing industry. She runs a factory where she works with wool and flax to make jerseys, baby clothes, and ponchos just to name a few woolen garments.

In Proverbs 31:49, she lays her hands on the spindle and works; she gets involved. She also makes coverings of tapestry, and her clothing is silk. She makes fine linen and sells it and delivers some of her goods to traders (Proverbs 31:22, 24). She is probably a manufacturer who owns a wholesale shop where traders come to buy in bulk. This woman is into serious business.

In Proverbs 31:14, we hear that her food is brought from afar. This woman could be an importer of food and wool. She could be a major player in the food industry for all we know. She lacks absolutely nothing.

Proverbs 31:15 mentions portions of meat the woman gives to her household and to her maids in the early hours of the morning. The probability is that she would have come from the slaughterhouse and hence brought liver to her home for breakfast. The woman could be in the meat industry as she helps her husband. The woman has maidens, which means she is an employer; whatever she is running is not a small affair. She is a woman of substance.

Let us arise as women and learn from such examples and other women around us to do things that will change our lives and even do things that will be our legacies after we are gone.

We go on to see the woman considering buying a field in Proverbs 31:16 and actually buying it to make it a vineyard. Here, the helper woman is into agriculture. The woman will till the land and produce substance, tangible crops, and real cash.

The areas into which this woman delves are usually male-dominated activities, but she is a helper who understands what God expects of her and is doing only what is expected of her. Thank God each woman has the divine ability to produce substance.

Unfortunately, women who choose to obey God, take the bull by the horns, and do things on their own are sometimes perceived as arrogant, proud, and disrespectful and as wives who override their husbands. This is especially true if they are helping husbands who are involved in lesser jobs, but it is not necessarily so.

It's not only society that holds that perception; at times, it is even the person being helped who is not comfortable with the prosperity of their helpers and their families. Isn't this strange? But the devil is always at work and wants to thwart whatever is precious to every woman and her family.

This poses a dilemma for women. What should they do? Should they try to please society, or should they follow what the Word of God says about them as helpers, women?

Women should continue to help regardless of what people might say or think. In the process of helping, if God blesses them with abundance, they should praise and thus glorify God's name.

A woman should be a fruitful helper. In Genesis, God instructed Adam and Eve to multiply as well as replenish and subdue the earth. This shows us that women were ordained to produce substance. They must not negate their duties. Helpers are very versatile creations of God. By God's grace, they are able to do great things. In 2 Corinthians 12:9, we read that God's grace is sufficient for us.

Chapter 4

Indirect but Vital Help

$\mathcal{M}$alachi 2:14 talks of a woman as a man's companion, a person who spends time with another, a friend.

It is vital that husband and wife spend time together, share, and get to know each other. That is a very essential prerequisite for effective helpers because they have to know and understand those they are helping to be effective and successful.

A helper should be a mediator, one who stands between God and her husband. In 1 Samuel 25:10, Nabal was extremely rude to David, a man of God. He purposefully refused to acknowledge

David. Abigail, Nabal's wife, heard of it and went out to look for David and plead with him not to shed Nabal's blood. That was granted, and God took Nabal's life shortly afterward because he had disrespected David. Thanks to Abigail, Nabal's life was spared for a while.

A helper fights for her husband's soul and his good in general. She seeks God's favor on him continually. She never gives up and never just watches because that is accepting defeat. She prays and seeks guidance from God.

A helper should be a prayer warrior. In Luke 2:36–38, we see a praying woman, Anna, a prophetess. She became a widow after seven years of marriage, but up to age eighty-four, she worshipped in the temple day and night. Prayer kept her going; prayer keeps a woman going strong.

In Exodus 15:20, Miriam and all the women of Israel took timbrels in their hands and went out singing, dancing, glorifying God, and magnifying their Savior because he had thrown the Egyptians and their horses into the sea. Here, we see helpers worshipping God and acknowledging that there is none like him, who rescued them from the Egyptians. A helper should be a worshipper. Helpers minister to men of God. Miriam was supporting her brother. She stands as a role model of a woman who was a person of influence and a worshipper.

In Luke 8:2, we also see certain women saving Jesus. It's the same spirit of helpers. Helpers do good for the men of God, i.e., pastors and leaders in their lives, their husbands, and other people. They are designed to serve.

The helper is a self-motivated person. In Proverbs 31:16, she considers buying a field and actually does so though other helpers would not follow through like that. She worked with her hands to attain her dreams. She pushed herself and did everything within her power to get a field, and then she did so.

A helper is a woman of faith. In 2 Timothy 1:5, Paul's letter to Timothy hails Timothy's grandmother Lois and mother Eunice for their genuine faith. Glory! A helper is able to say, "For with God nothing shall be impossible" (Luke 1:37), and she is able to speak as if she has what she hopes to have by faith. Hebrews 11:1 says, "Faith is the substance of things hoped for, the evidence of things not seen."

A helper should always be full of faith and stay calm and unmoved in all situations. A helper should always be positive even with tears in her eyes; she should smile and say all is well as per the promise of the Lord. A helper stands on God's promises.

A helper is an unselfish and prayerful person. Esther was such a person. She did not ignore all the Jews because King Ahasuerus had made her queen. Instead, she acted boldly and went into the king's chamber before the king called her. Esther, her maids, and all the Jews under her instructions fasted and prayed day and night for three days regardless of her comfort. In Esther 4:16, Esther made a commitment to see the king although it was against the law and although it could cost her her life. A helper should be a very bold person because at times, she can face life-threatening situations. But Esther knew who she was. She also knew the powers bestowed on her when she was made queen; that is why she could go to the king. Helpers should always know they have powers bestowed on them by God to help the men in their lives.

A helper has good influence over her husband. Wherever her man is, she is there too to put order and organize his life. It is also crucial that a helper be a spirit-filled person, someone who is very sensitive, someone who knows the person she is helping extremely well. She knows him so well that the moment he walks into the house, she can tell if he had had a rough day, and she immediately helps him relax and think clearly without stressing him more.

Chapter 5

Why a Man Needs Help

Who needs help? That is the question we might ask, but according to God, every man needs a helper and help—no exceptions. By their state, men qualify to have helpers. That is why we see that every man, even one whom we least expect to do so, manages to find a wife.

Though he has a helper, he has duties he is expected to fulfill for his family and at times the nation. Ephesians 5:23 talks of the husband being the head of the wife as Christ is the head of the church and the Savior of the body. It is therefore a man's responsibility to head and run his household; God expects that of him. He needs a helper to head the home, and that is when the woman comes in. The woman is answerable to the man, and the man is answerable to God.

The man in Proverbs 31:2 is said to be well known in the gates where he sat among the elders of the land. It does not say he was an elder. He could have been one, but he could also have been just an ordinary man who hung around all the time and was not gainfully employed, but he had a helper who ran his life so well that his dress was outstanding.

Proverbs 31:11 talks of the heart of this man (husband) safely trusting his wife such that he has no need of spoil—goods taken by force from people or places. It looks as if he did not even have to work. The Bible says he sat among the elders. He knew his wife would look after all the affairs of him home, educate their children, dress them, and put food on the table. All was under control because his helper was in control. Indeed, she was blessed that her husband appreciated her, and even the children called her blessed (Proverbs 31:28).

Proverbs 13:22 says, "A good man leaves an inheritance for his children's children." This man provides materially for his family. The man must be a great worker who is able to leave inheritances for even his children's children's grandchildren. What a challenge! A man therefore needs a helper to plan and work with.

Ephesians 5:25 says, "Husbands, love your wives even as Christ also loved the church and gave himself for it." Here, we see that man is tasked to love his wife. Loving one's wife is not always simple or easy because if it were so, Paul would not have been inspired by the Holy Spirit to write that. The number of broken marriages and divorces we see and hear about daily shows how difficult it can be to keep love going.

Many times because of what happens around us, we wonder if love is an illusion, but we should thank God, who taught us what love is. He loved us when we were sinners and took it upon himself to die for us. In John 15:12 is the commandment that we love one another as Christ has loved us. A man needs a helper to teach him unconditional love, which the helper always has toward her children.

Fathers, do not provoke your children to wrath; bring them up in the nurture and admonition of the Lord. We see that fathers are expected to train their children in godly ways and correct them when they err. Proverbs 3:12 says that the Lord corrects those he loves just as a father does with children in which he delights. The helper, the wife, will instill biblical principles in her children because she spends more time with them.

In Titus 2, we see that men are to be temperate and self-controlled. These attributes will help them to be good, loving husbands full of patience and tolerance.

We see in Genesis 26:22 that Isaac and his men were digging wells as had been done by Abraham. The man here is portrayed as a provider. He made sure all the people and animals had water. They were nomads, so that was not always an easy task, but Isaac did it.

The Old Testament is full of wars and men who went to war. They were expected to defend their nations and stand in the gap. Praying for their leaders and nations is another way men can show their acceptance and support of their leaders and nations.

Chapter 6

Young, Unmarried Women

$\mathcal{G}$od loves you single as you are, so do not rush into marriage. Do not fret, do not stress. There is a time and season for everything.

Enjoy your youth. Your time to put on the robe of helper will come. Your only God-prescribed duty at this station of your life is to fear and serve God. Ecclesiastes 12:13 says, "Fear God and keep his commandments, for this is the whole duty of man." We are to seek righteousness and please the Lord as Paul wrote in 1 Corinthians 7:32: "He that is unmarried cares for the things that belong to the Lord, how he may please the Lord." As you seek to know the Lord, engage Him in your future. Ask for a godly husband, a man who worships God in spirit and truth.

God is a God of specifics. When you ask him for a husband, be very specific and tell God exactly what you want from and in a husband. Pray for him from head to toe. God is faithful; He grants us the desires of our hearts. Psalm 37:4 says that if we delight ourselves in the Lord, he will give us our hearts' desires.

Ask the Lord for a husband, but get on with your life. In Genesis 29, Rachel was looking after her father's sheep; she was minding her own business and not worrying about her seemingly lateness in marriage when divine things started to happen. People came from far to marry her. So fret not, young woman—your husband is there somewhere. In the fullness of time, things you will not even understand will start to happen and you will get married.

When he comes, you will know him. This is because there is something called marrying right. Esau married Judith, but he did not marry right. Genesis 26:35 says it was a grief to Isaac and Rebekah. This is why it is crucial that you seek counsel of the Lord so you will marry right. It is advisable to get a partner from your own; birds of a feather flock together. Marry from your own nation, race, culture, and faith.

Samson, an Israelite, married Delilah, a Philistine, and things did not work out well. Choose from among your own; that will minimize friction. In 2 Corinthians 6:14, the unmarried are advised not to be equally yoked to unbelievers. Believers should marry fellow believers; they should marry in their own faith.

You must also be conscious of who you are all the time. Know yourself very well—your strengths and weaknesses especially if you are born again. A little maid who waited on Naaman's wife knew herself and her people. She was in a strange land and in captivity, but she knew her God. She told her mistress about the prophet in Samaria who was mightily used by her God. The girl was instrumental in Naaman's healing. She did not forget who she was even though she was many miles from her home and in bondage.

Pray for yourself as well. Pray that patience may reign in your life until the right person comes along. Pray you will not face the devil's evil manipulation, delays, or hindrances to your getting married. Stand firmly against the spirits of discouragement, fear, worry, and frustration especially as you grow older before Mr. Right comes along. Seek God lest you are tempted to get involved in ungodly relationships or do ungodly things.

Equip yourself with the skills you need to keep your home and improve yourself. As prescribed in Titus 2, you will have to be sober, calm, good, and obedient, and you will have to love your husband and children. You will have to be discreet and have sound speech. All these attributes will not come automatically just because you marry. You will have to learn to be good and handle the chores necessary to qualify you as a good helper and wife. This is the time to enroll in baking, cooking, sewing, and interior decorating classes.

Buy one or two recipe books. Get a driver's license. Making yourself knowledgeable of such skills is always handy and is in fact a necessity.

This is also your time to look good. If maidens during King Ahasuerus's time in Esther 2:12 took twelve months to purify themselves with oil of myrrh, sweet smells, and other things to purify themselves, we all need to attend a finishing school where we are taught grooming and etiquette. Looking good is not as easy as we might think, but a few hints here and there will make a world of difference to the finished product, and in this case, you are the product.

Add value to yourself in all ways. Improve yourself academically. Let the sky be the limit. A helper does endless calculations; if you miscalculate, your family will suffer. Become knowledgeable of how to conduct business, how to approach people effectively, how to fund whatever you need, and many other things. Knowledge gives you power, so acquire as much of it as you can.

In Luke 8:3, we read of women who ministered to Jesus with their substance. Most of us fall into this category in our churches. We are there to minister to the servants of God with our substance and God through giving to those in need. It is important that we have the skills and education necessary to minister to the servants of God, our families, and the needy among us. Proverbs 31:20 reads, "She stretches her hand to the poor, she reaches forth her hands to the needy." As women, we are expected to have tangible substance we can give others.

If the totality of your life depends on finding a husband, improve yourself. Christian D. Larson wrote, "Give so much time to the improvement of yourself that you have no time to criticise others."[2]

Ladies, including you young ladies, seek to improve yourselves in all areas of life. The earlier the unmarried learn this the better, because after marriage, there will be more family members to look after and responsibilities to go with that.

I exhort you to find an older, biblical woman who will mentor you as you pursue spiritual growth so that by the time you get married, you

---

[2] Larson C.D., **Your forces and how to use them**, CreateSpace Independent Publishing Platform (July 29, 2008), Chapter 1, Pg. 6

will be a mature Christian. Mentorship never ends. It is better to start being mentored before you want to get married rather than when you have a partner because at that time, your partiality to issues will be compromised. An older woman will mentor you throughout life. Learning never ends.

Chapter 7

Dos and Don'ts for Every Woman

It is obvious that as a helper, you will not be perfect when you execute your tasks, but be encouraged because no one other than God is perfect. Be encouraged too because your position is God ordained and his grace is sufficient for you and every woman.

Challenges will arise here; things will go wrong or not work out well in your marriage, but never look at your shortfalls and blame yourself. Romans 8:1 reads, "There is therefore now no condemnation to them which are in Christ Jesus who walk not after the flesh but after the spirit." Are you born again? Do you do everything for the Lord? There is no condemnation on you. Don't ever blame yourself when things are not smooth sailing. Self-blame is the tool the devil uses to destroy you.

Most times, some of your deeds are not even mistakes; they are merely perceptions. People perceive things differently. The person you are trying to help might perceive your good intentions as ways to drag him down. The devil is a liar. He can hijack your husband's thoughts and make him think you are his worst enemy. Remember that we are at war and wrestle not against flesh and blood but against principalities, powers, rulers of darkness, and spiritual wickedness in high places (Ephesians 6:12).

Though we are always at war, we should never become tired of doing good. Galatians 6:9 advises us not to be weary in doing good for in due season we will reap if we faint not. As long as we have the ability, we should work toward our goals because the Lord has put the divine ability in us—every woman—to attain great heights.

Also remember that the devil roars like a lion trying to threaten us; if we don't stand firm and strong, we might fall by the wayside. That is what the devil wants to see. Never get confused; when you pray, fast, and believe God totally for deliverance or restoration but nothing seems to happen, the devil will raise his ugly head and try to dampen and kill your spirit. Stay focused. Keep on believing God for what you want. Raise your faith. Hebrews 11:1 says, "Now faith is the substance of things hoped for, evidence of things not seen." Keep on believing God until you see results.

Do not be blind. Pray for spiritual eyes, and be like other women of faith who died believing. They believed they had gotten things from God. Hebrew 11:11 says, "Through faith Sara herself received strength to conceive seed and was delivered of a child when she was past age, because she judged him faithfully who had promised"!

Faith in God gives us strength to overcome the seemingly impossible things that happen to us, so we should never give up! We have a Father who specializes in impossibilities. Our God cares. Luke 18:27 says, "The things which are impossible with men are possible with God."

If your husband is weak, he has failed to help himself. You as his helpmate cannot change him even though you see what needs to be put right. Your only alternative is to bring him and his problem before God, who has the power and ability to change him.

When you are blamed for things that go wrong in your family, do not take offense. In Genesis 3:12, we read that after Adam ate the forbidden fruit, he told God, "The woman whom thou gave to be with me, she gave me of the tree and I did eat." Adam could have not eaten the fruit; he had the power to say no. He knew the rules God had given him, but he tried to push the blame on Eve.

Expect this tendency as a helper, but do not let it dampen your spirit. Keep on helping the Adam in your life regardless of what he says or thinks about you.

Always forgive. Never hold grudges. That can be extremely difficult, but God expects us to forgive. In the Lord's Prayer, Jesus taught us to pray saying, "Forgive us our trespasses, as we forgive those who trespass against us." In Matthew 6:12, we learn that if we forgive men their trespasses, our heavenly Father will forgive us. We are not perfect; we need God to forgive our sins. Forgiving others is a key to our own forgiveness. Regardless of how much we have been wronged, we should learn to forgive because forgiveness is medicinal; it heals our hearts and makes us happy. We feel good, and we can tune in to God very easily in prayer and spirit.

Do not partake of your helper's shortfalls by getting angry, not forgiving, staying bitter, taking revenge, or any other bad things you might want to do. Seeking revenge is a sin it itself.

Never compromise your salvation because of the person you are trying to help. Judgment Day will surely come; 1 Corinthians 3:13 says, "Every man's work shall be made manifest for the day shall declare it because it shall be revealed by fire and the fire shall try every man's work of what sort it is." So do not allow anything to steal your salvation; instead, be consumed with zeal for the Lord.

Psalm 69:9 says, "For the zeal of thine house has eaten me up and the reproaches of them that reproached thee are fallen upon me." Be zealous to the point that others leave you alone because they know that when it comes to the Lord's work, you do not compromise and that your God is always first.

Never allow confusion to rule you. Find scriptures to explain each situation you face. In Luke 12, the Prodigal Son squandered his father's money on prostitutes, but thank God, when he came back to his senses, he went back to the father. Some people act badly when they lose their senses. As a helper, you are to stay sober all the time and never lose your senses.

Search the scriptures to be wise. Be knowledgeable of secular things as well. Another profitable way of assimilating the Word is to preach to others the Word that relates to what you are going through. As you read the scriptures and teach the Word, you will minister to yourself as well. God is gracious; he preaches to you as you teach. You will overcome by the word of your testimony.

Never look down on yourself because you are special. Psalm 139:14 says you were wonderfully and fearfully made by God. Encourage yourself and tell yourself good things about yourself. The woman with an issue of blood did that in Matthew 9:21: "For she said in her heart if I may but touch this garment I shall be whole." Tell yourself that you are God's special child. There is power in telling yourself what the scriptures say about you and what you believe is correct. Do not just stop there; take it a step further and do things to look and feel good—things like makeup or losing weight are important.

Never be a loner. The world is full of righteous people, so find them, network with them, and enjoy them. Some might be living with their husbands but feel terribly lonely because their sense of sharing and oneness has vanished. Despite this, find godly people to relate to. Just the godly conversation Elizabeth and Mary made the baby in Elizabeth's womb jump; their conversation activated the Holy Spirit, and things started happening.

Malachi 3:16 says, "Then they that feared the Lord spoke often one to another and the Lord hearkened and heard it and a book of remembrance was written before him." The Lord takes note of our godly conversations. Find those who can encourage you in the Lord, pray with you, and give you the adult company you need. There is always someone out there who has time for you, but the onus is on you to find them.

We are never alone because we have a shepherd who watches over us (Psalm 23: 1). Any sheep with a shepherd it is not alone; we Christians are never alone because our Father is always with us.

You might be ashamed at what is going on in your life or marriage, but you are only being human, and it shows you care. For your sake, find someone to talk to. If you are not ready to talk to someone, talk to trees or the walls of your private room. That is very healthy, and after all, the walls have ears and eyes; they see when things are happening, and sooner or later, you will realize you are not alone. Some people are going through the same as you are if not worse, but you can learn that only if you talk to other people.

Sing to and praise the Lord, who says he dwells in our praises. In that way, you invite him into your issues and challenges. Encourage yourself by the Word of God, and confess the Word all the time. Write Bible verses on stickers and attach them everywhere you look—the kitchen, office, and bathroom. Put them in all the strategic places where you can read the positive confessions and scriptures as you encourage yourself. Write promises in your phone and read them daily and regularly to encourage yourself. Make daily declarations of what you want to see happen in your life. If you are contemplating suicide, stop pursuing that thought as it is a no-go area! It is not a solution because if you died, your problems would remain unsolved.

Face your issues squarely! Jesus came that you might have life in abundance (John 10:10). God created you to be above, not below. You can manage the situation. Daniel 2:21 says, "And he changes the times and the seasons." It is only a short season you are going through; it will surely change. Rejoice in the Lord (Philippians 4:4); in everything, praise the Lord. Despite how bleak things might look, search for positive things you can praise God for no matter how trivial they might be. Count your blessings one by one. Praise the Lord for the lovely sun, your job, the food you have on your plate, your children and friends, the wisdom he gives you, your house, car, grandchildren, a good night's sleep, your neighbors, good health, and for many other things. That will give you hope and a reason to go on.

Though your situation might be contrary to what the Word of God says, continue to praise the Lord. Read your Bible; sing hymns to yourself that confess what the Word of God says about your situation to keep yourself focused. Remember that it is all about you, not others. You can experience the very best God has to offer.

Chapter 8

Communication Helps

$\mathcal{A}$ helper who wants to enjoy success in executing her duties must be in dialogue with the person she is helping. Communication in marriage is vital; it makes or breaks most relationships.

But before wise helpers communicate with their partners, they must ask themselves, *What exactly do I mean here?* Helpers must process their issues and even rehearse what they want to communicate to make sure they use appropriate words and tone.

By the nature of their jobs, teachers tend to overemphasize their points when talking. Unfortunately, that does not always go down well with spouses, so tone matters very much. Helpers must think ahead when confronted with challenges and be able to deal with issues from various perspectives.

Communication is a two-way process between the helper and the helped. There must be a transmission of thoughts, ideas, and feelings from one mind to another. Because it involves two parties, communication can be very complex. The person being helped might refuse to cooperate. Some people do not take time to listen to their spouses. It is very sad, but when someone takes such an extreme stand, there is nothing the helper can do except to wait on the Lord for the day they are able to discuss issues pertaining to their lives together.

Silence can cause larger problems. If the silence is genuine and not the result of anger or a grudge held, all is well. However, that fact should be communicated to avoid misinterpretation by the other spouse.

Some people, however, are not natural communicators; they find it hard to communicate. In such an instant, a couple should work on finding ways to communicate. In addition to this, they can pray and hope that by God's grace, they will plot the way forward amicably.

If you have issues with your husband, find a quiet place and time to talk. Avoid discussions in front of children or when you go to bed. By that time, both of you will be tired, so not much constructive talk can take place. Go to a beautiful park, admire the flowers together, and then talk. Go to a place where you used to meet when you were dating to revive thoughts and feelings of your first love.

A couple should be able to discuss anything freely. Couples who are able to talk to each other about issues will dream together as they journey together in their marriage.

As a couple, do not discuss just bits of information about minor issues; talk about those important and difficult topics. If for whatever reason you two cannot discuss an issue and come to an agreement and you leave the issue hanging in the air, revisit the issue later to come to a conclusion on it. Do not allow pending issues to create tension at home. Blocked communication can build up pressure at home. Iron out your differences and enjoy each other. Remember that if you and your husband disagree, that is not a fight; it is just the result of your seeing things differently.

Always be kind and polite when you are discussing important issues; do not point fingers at one another. Do not attack or engage in controlling comments; speak in a way that shows your interest in your husband. Proverbs 15:1 reads, "A soft answer turns away wrath, but grievous words stir up anger."

A helper should be a person of soft words; she should not engage in the blame game. Once a blame game starts, it is difficult to solve issues amicably. What I cannot overemphasize is that both partners should talk tactfully to one another.

As a good helper, be reminded of Proverbs 21:9: "It is better to dwell in a corner of the housetop, than with a brawling woman in a house." Men are not comfortable with the way some women speak. Some women use harsh, unkind words. A helper should be able to tame her tongue.

Hand in glove with communication is listening. A helper should be a good listener, someone who does not brush her partner aside or take him for a joke when they share their concerns. A good listener inclines toward the person speaking to let him know she is actively engaged in the conversation. A good listener takes note of every detail of the story before trying to assist. She asks clarifying questions to make sure she has heard what her partner is saying.

Listeners' eyes and facial expressions are important in communication. Listeners should make eye contact during conversations and take care that their facial expressions show alertness, caring, and interest. Gestures like rolling eyes are cues that listeners are bored or do not care about what the speaker is saying. Avoid such gestures at all costs.

Avoid using the word *you* and pointing fingers; those are confrontational. Rather, use the word *we* when putting a message across. On the other hand, crossing your arms over your chest signifies to listeners that you do not agree with them and are not willing to listen to what they are saying. Fiddling with your hands or crossing your legs imparts cues that you are not interested in what is going on. Keeping still while listening may not be easy, but it lets speakers know you care about what they are saying.

Some people opt for giving others the silent treatment, but that is still a form of communication; it expresses a passive-aggressive attitude, a control mechanism. Silence communicates a strong message. Instead of engaging in the silent treatment, couples should learn to talk to each other and resolve their issues.

Do not try to predict your partner's thoughts. Do not assume anything. State your thoughts clearly and honestly; that results in less confusion and frustration. Discussing helps couples reach the point that they can share the same vision. If they need to, they can take their issues together to the Lord in prayer.

More interesting still, even when you disagree on some issues as a couple, when you kneel in prayer, you can be specific with your request to God because you know your partner's stand.

Talk to each other with no secrecy, deceit, and lying, which breaks trust. Little lies turn into big lies, and they can damage a marriage permanently.

Good communication is vital in a relationship. In Ephesians 4:29, Paul wrote, "Let no corrupt communication proceed out of your mouth, but that which is good to the use of edifying, that it may minister grace unto the hearers." What you say should be meant to build up others; maybe it will be to correct them, but it should never be meant to put them down or inflict pain on them.

Communication gives you a chance to let your companion know exactly what you like and dislike. Never assume your partner knows what you like; tell him and discuss it honestly but never rudely. Do it politely to avoid hurting him. That will make your time together light, breezy, and fun, and it will avoid or clear up misunderstandings and prevent mistrust. Transparency is crucial, and it is brought about by communication.

If for some reason a couple hurts each other, they should overcome the hurt by talking about the hurtful issue. Husbands should remember that wives are weaker vessels and treat them as such. In 1 Peter 3:7, husbands are exhorted to deal with their wives with intelligence; failure in this matter will hinder God from hearing their prayers.

Be sympathetic to your partner. If he has a perspective that differs from yours, take time to explain yourself and understand him to avoid rocking the boat. This is vital because when the communication flow is stormy, that can cause danger and destruction. Avoid such communication storms by talking calmly and frankly; encourage one another, and avoid criticizing each other.

If an argument erupts, one party needs to scale down the temper politely. Be the bigger person because it is not always easy to swallow one's pride. You must also learn to apologize if you are wrong.

Some people have a habit of keeping score, but that is a habit to avoid. Once you start doing so, you open the door for the other person to do the same, and months or even years later, you pull your scorecards out. Find an amicable way of solving problems by communicating effectively, an essential skill.

Good helpers read their partner's minds as well as know their own; Psalm 51:10 reads, "Create in me a clean heart oh Lord." At times, we humans entertain dirty thoughts and minds, so we should take stock of our minds and thoughts at all times so that when we communicate, we do so constructively and speak our love to others. When we can read our partners' minds, we will be able to help them in the most suitable ways.

Communicate your loving thoughts with acts of service and gifts. That bunch of flowers, a surprise birthday party or present, a special chocolate bar, and going the extra mile for your spouse do not go unnoticed. All these forms of communication strengthen the bond between you.

Couples should learn from the onset of their marriage to pray for each other. When they experience a problem, it can become difficult and even impossible for them to pray as they once did.

For instance, if you prayed for your partner to get a decent job and he did, but then he neglects his responsibilities at home, it is almost impossible to pray to God to take that job away; it's difficult to reverse ones' prayers about someone.

Communication might seem complex, but God, who created marriage, is on your side. Just continually connect with him and ask him for wisdom and guidance in your marriage walk.

Chapter 9

The ABC's of a Helper

$\mathcal{T}$he following and many others are the attributes of helpers that help them to be as perfect as they can be. As you read these, you will discover that the attributes are closely interlinked.

The helper is a very special being because she is Christlike.

A—Alert. A helper knows she has an enemy she has to fight day and night. The enemy seeks to kill and destroy her family through various ways—breaking up marriages, physical death, turning children against parents—you name it (John 10:10). The helper works tirelessly to counter the devil's attacks and asks for God's protection for herself and her family. She prays unceasingly (1 Thessalonians 5:17).

B—Blessing. The woman is a blessing to all people around her—husband, children, relatives, and community (Proverbs 31:28). All they see in her is good, and they shower her with praises.

C—Calm. She is in control of herself and situations in her home. Proverbs 21:9 talks of a brawling woman who talks endlessly until the husband sees fit to dwell in a corner of the housetop. A helper should never be found wanting; she knows what to say and when to say it. She is disciplined.

D—Diligent. The helper works, and she knows no boundaries. She knits. She imports food. She runs a butchery. She is into farming. She is a marketer who sells linen and girdles. She is a businesswoman for sure (Proverbs 31:13–24).

E—Enemy. She is conscious of who her enemy is. It is not her mother-in-law. It is not her husband either. It is the devil. Genesis 3:15 tells us God put enmity between the serpent and the woman. The helper is therefore at war fighting the devil.

F—Forgiveness. She forgives everybody no matter how difficult that might be; that is what our Lord Jesus taught us to do in Matthew 6:14–15. Not forgiving cuts us off from God. When we pray, he does not hear our prayers.

G—Gentle. Gentleness is one of the fruits of the spirit and is the cousin of calmness (Galatians 6: 22). God is a gentle man.

H—Humble. A helper humbles herself before God first and then her husband. In 1 Peter 5:6, we read that God wants to lift us up as women and requires humility from us.

I—Integrity. She is honest to herself, husband, family, and the whole world. Lack of integrity leads to death. We read of Sapphira and Ananias in Acts 5:1–10 who died in the temple because they lied to the men of God.

J—Joyful. The helper knows where her joy comes from—the Lord. The joy of the Lord is her strength (Nehemiah 8:10). She knows the benefits of joy too. Joy attracts the favor and protection of the Lord, so she is deliberately joyful (Psalm 5:11–12). She is a joyful person because she stays in the presence of the Lord. Joy creates a warm and healthy environment for her family.

K—Keeper of her home. She keeps good care of her family and home. She is concerned about the well-being of her family (Titus 2). She is a kind person like Dorcas. She cares about all people, even her neighbors.

L—Loving. She has the nature of God, who loves us despite what he knows about us. In John 13: 27–38, we learn that Jesus knew Judas Iscariot would betray him, but he loved him to the end. He loved like a little child; so should a helper. A helper also loves instruction.

M—Mother. In Mark 3:35, Jesus said that whoever did the will of God was his mother and sister. A helper is therefore a mother of Jesus because she is zealous for the things of the house of God.

N—Nurse. A helper is a gentle person who cherishes all people as much as she does her children (1 Thessalonians 2:7). She nurtures them until they are independent. A helper looks after others.

O—Obeys. She obeys God first and then her husband. On earth, despite being God, Jesus obeyed his Father even unto death (Philippians 2:8).

P—Peacemaker. She strives to be at peace with all people including her in-laws because peacemakers are blessed. Matthew 5:9 says peacemakers will be called the children of God.

Q—Quiet. In 1 Thessalonians 4:11, we read, "And that you study to be quiet, and to do your own business and to work with your own hands, as we commanded you." She quietly studies the Word of God and minds her own business. She is calm and gentle.

R—Reverences God. God is the Alpha and Omega (Revelations 22:13). She respects God for the great things he does in her and her family's lives. She fears God and does not devise ungodly ways of running her marriage; she strives to do good all the time.

S—Shepherd. She shepherds her family as did the good shepherd in John 10:11, who gave her life for her sheep. She is also a sober person because like a shepherd, she wants to take good care of her family. Sober shepherds will be able to protect their sheep (1 Peter 5:8).

T—Teacher. She teaches her family the Word of God all the time—when sitting in her house, when walking, when lying down, and more so after rising up (Deuteronomy 10:19). She applies the Word of God to her life, and that is evident every day; her family learns from how she runs her life.

U—Upright. She is an upright person who pleases God all the time through prayer; she is a useful asset in God's kingdom. Her prayers please God (Proverbs 15:8). She is righteous because righteousness pleases God.

V—Victor. She is a victorious person who never gives up. She has the nature of Jesus, who won the final victory over Satan when he descended into hell (Revelation 1:18). She carries that same spirit when dealing with issues in her home.

W—Wise. She is full of godly wisdom as she cares for her home and family; she keeps her home and family together (Proverbs 14:1). Her wisdom is the mind of God revealed to her because she seeks to know God.

X—'Xemplary. She is a doer of the word because she knows she is a letter read by all people great and small. In 2 Corinthians 3:2, we read that we are our own epistles written in our hearts that are known and read by all; they are not written with ink but with the Spirit of the Living God, not on tablets of stone but on fleshly tablets.

Y—Yoke bearer. The helper knows all the devices of the devil. She stands in the gap and fights for her family. She cries to the Lord to break all inherited spiritual yokes and other things that might be weighing down any in her family (Matthew 11:28–29).

Z—Zealous. She is filled with a zeal to serve God. Like David, she says that the zeal of the things of God's house has overtaken her. She would rather be a doorkeeper in the house of her God than dwell in the tents of wickedness. She wants to be in the presence of God all the time.

Conclusion

In Genesis 1:31, we read that God saw everything he had made and declared it good; this included woman. There is no mismatch in marriages; couples were designed by God to complement each other. God put into each woman a divine capacity and ability to be an effective helper.

Being a helper is not easy, but God ordained women to be effective helpers. Many times, their help might not be appreciated or acknowledged, but glory be to God because they can take their challenges to him in prayer.

Always remember that in God's business, there are no mistakes. Every couple is perfect in the eyes of God.

Philippians 4:6 says, "Be careful for nothing but in everything by prayer and supplication with thanksgiving let your requests be made known unto God." God is good; he wants to hear all our requests, and being our father, he always does something about our requests. Going to him constantly to recommit ourselves and our husbands to God and asking him for his help or intervention shows us the way forward. Philippians 4:13, "I can do all things through Christ who strengthens me" should be every woman's slogan because women can do all things.

Women, do you realize how special you are? You are part of God's plan for your husbands' and families' salvation. Help your husbands discover themselves in the Lord if they are not born again. In 1 Corinthians 7:14, we read about the unbelieving husband being sanctified by the wife. Your husbands can be made holy because you have accepted Jesus as your personal Savior.

When as a woman you bring joy and harmony into your home and family, you are happy, and you will see the fruits of your labor—your dreams coming true. You need to have a personal relationship with God so you can commune with him as friend to friend, as father and daughter. That can be achieved only after you have accepted

Jesus as your personal Savior. To do so, I invite you to say this prayer wholeheartedly;

"Lord God, I come to you in the name of Jesus Christ. I admit that I am a sinner and cannot save myself. Your Word says 'For all have sinned and come short of the glory of God' (Romans 3:23). I thank you because your Word also says that whoever believes in God will not perish but have eternal life (John 3:16).

"I choose you. I ask you, Jesus, to come into my heart to be the Lord of my life and forgive me of my sins. I declare that I am a child of God. I now have Christ dwelling in me. I now walk in the consciousness of my new life in Christ Jesus, amen."

You are now born again, and you can now claim the promises in the Bible because you are now a child of God. As a helper, you are no longer doing it alone; God is on your side, the winning side.

Such are the challenges of a helper and hence the inclusion of the phrase "dying together is victory" in the first chapter. One goes through many challenges, but by God's grace, many women are doing their duty very successfully.

Always be proud to be a woman, a dynamic vessel specially designed by God to help a man. Ecclesiastes 4:9 says, "Two are better than one, because they have a good reward for their labour."

Be blessed as you execute your God-ordained duties!

Notes

Notes

Notes

Notes

Notes

Notes

Notes

Printed in the United States
By Bookmasters